Somebody
Special
To God

Jerry Savelle

You're Somebody Special To God

by Jerry Savelle

8th Printing
Over 100,000 in Print

You're Somebody Special To God

ISBN 0-89274687-4
Unless otherwise stated,
all Scripture quotations are taken from
the *King James Version* of the Bible.

Jerry Savelle Ministries International
P.O. Box 748
Crowley, Texas 76036

God's Prized-Possession

Have you ever felt insecure? Insecure about your abilities, your appearance, your job, your personality, your life? Have you ever felt unloved and worthless? "I'm not attractive." "I can't do all the things that person can do." "I'm not good enough!" "Nothing good ever happens in my life." "I'm a failure."

If your mind is filled with thoughts of worthlessness, shame, embarrassment and low self-esteem, then it's time to get rid of that insecurity!

"How can I get rid of insecurity that's been there my whole life?" By realizing that YOU are God's most prized-possession! If God had to choose the finest thing He ever created - He'd say YOU! Yes, you! You are somebody special to God.

Those thoughts and feelings are lies from the Devil aimed at getting you so down on yourself that you will never experience God's best for your life. You'll always feel that you're "just not good enough" so why would God want to bless you? God does not have one child who is not good enough to receive His love.

There are a lot of people who never enjoy victories in their lives because of such low self-esteem. Jesus said that we are to love one another even as we love ourselves. If you don't like YOU, how are you ever going to like somebody else?

Low self-esteem is a result of a lack of knowledge. The reason so many Christians live way below their privileges as a child of God is because they don't know that they are highly favored of God.

In Psalm 8:3-5, the psalmist is reflecting on the greatness of God and writes, *When I consider thy heavens, the work of thy fingers, the moon and the stars, which thou hast ordained: What is man that thou art mindful of him? and the son of man, that thou visitest him? For thou hast made him a little lower than the angels, and hast crowned him with glory and honour.*

In this particular scripture, the psalmist is overwhelmed at just how marvelous and magnificent God is and His ability to create the universe. Have you ever just stopped and looked around at God's creation? Just go look at the Grand Canyon some time. It's overwhelming. We get so accustomed to the things around us, but if you take the time to just look at the sky or the sunset and think that God created that - it's amazing!

The psalmist is saying, "Lord, You're so magnificent and creative, why would You have anything to do with man? Why did You create man?" And the Lord is saying that you are His most prized-possession! In fact, in the mind of God, you are His prized-possession above the stars, above the moon, above the heavens, above all His handiwork.

Just like an artist with all the wonderful, creative pieces he designs, there's always this one prized-possession. That's the way God feels about YOU!

Now, religion doesn't teach us that. Religion wants us to stay in a sinful state. *All have sinned and come short of the glory of God.* Well, that's true, but that's the reason Jesus came, because all sinned and fell short of the glory of God, but God didn't leave us that way, praise God. He sent Jesus to redeem us from Adam's transgression, and from the curse of the law, and because the blood of Jesus worked, we're not that old man anymore.

Nothing you did in your past could be so bad that God wouldn't forgive you. You are washed by the blood of Jesus, and made a new creation in Christ Jesus. You have the nature of Almighty God!

You are of a royal family. In the natural, you may have some folks in your family that you're not too proud of, but I'm talking about in the spirit realm, your ancestry goes all the way back to God. The blood of Jesus flows through your veins. You've got a crown on your head that can't be seen with the natural eye, but it's there, and you need to walk in that honor.

You are somebody special to God! Don't consider yourself a worm in the sight of God. "We're just pilgrims." No, we're not! "We're just worms in His sight." No, we're not. You better not be a worm, the Devil will come by and eat thee!

You can't be a worm in the sight of God. If you are, then that would mean the blood of Jesus didn't work, and I wouldn't dare say the blood of Jesus didn't work. It worked, praise God.

Very importantly, you've got to keep it all balanced. You can't become highminded and have the attitude of you're somebody special because of what you did or because of who you are. That has nothing to do with it. Without Jesus, you're nothing! You have no merits, you didn't earn this favor, you didn't earn this honor, Jesus earned it for you. But, because He did, you need to walk in it.

When you begin to see yourself the way God sees you (crowned with glory and honor), then you'll begin to expect success. You'll expect every adversity to turn into a victory. You'll expect to have authority over your circumstances. Why? Because you're God's prized-possession.

Preferential Treatment

There are so many people who don't expect good things to happen to them. In fact, people really get mad at me because I'm too positive. I'm not just a positive thinker. I'm not dealing with the power of positive thinking, I'm dealing with the power of revelation knowledge. When you have something revealed to you from the Word of God, it causes you to become positive. You'll have a positive attitude.

Doubt and insecurity will vanish as you become more and more conscious of just how much favor and honor you have been given by God. John 12:26 says, ...*if any man serve me, him will my Father honour.*

If you've chosen to serve Jesus, then Jesus Himself said because of your decision, *My Father will honor you.* Hallelujah! When you're honored by someone, that's preferential treatment.

You should begin to walk in authority - walk in dominion. You should expect to have authority over the circumstances that seem to be controlling your life. You should expect, with the Name of Jesus and the Word of God, to change those circumstances into something that turns out to be good in your life.

When you truly know that God has crowned you with glory and honor, then you will walk in an expectancy of good things happening in your life.

We haven't been walking in the kind of blessings we're entitled to. When you're honored by someone, that opens doors that men say are shut. When you're honored and favored of God, that entitles you to certain privileges that other folks don't enjoy.

Ephesians 6:24 says, *Grace* (or favor) *be with all them that love our Lord Jesus Christ in sincerity.* What is another definition for the word *grace?* "Unmerited favor"- something you didn't earn, it was a gift of God. So, when you see the word "grace," you can interchange it with the word "favor."

What is *favor?* Something granted out of good will. A gift bestowed as a token of regard, love or friendliness, preferential treatment. You can't be so good that finally God will say, "you're so good, you've now earned favor." <u>It is a gift from God.</u>

Don't get mad at some believers because they're blessed. You can be just as blessed, if you're not. Don't get mad when you hear testimonies of wonderful things happening in a believer's life. The Bible says that God is no respecter of persons, so that means the same preferential treatment that they get, you can have it too.

Obviously, if you don't have a revelation of it, then you can't walk in it. A lack of knowledge will cause you to live way below your privileges. But once you have revelation of how special you are to God, then praise God you will be able to walk in favor.

The Object Of God's Affection

Do you feel loved? It's a wonderful thing knowing you're loved. Knowing that there is somebody out there that loves you makes you feel good inside. But if you feel unloved and feel that there is absolutely no one out there who even cares about you, then the lies of the Devil are working in you and creating a deep feeling of loneliness. But listen to this: Even greater than a human being expressing love to you, the Lord says in Numbers 6:25,26 that He will ... *make his face shine upon thee, and be gracious unto thee: The Lord lift up his countenance upon thee, and give thee peace.*

What is He saying? You are the object of God's affection. If you were the only human being alive on the planet, God would have sent Jesus to die for you. That's how much you're loved by the Father. I believe some of you are going to experience a real deliverance simply because you've realized you're loved and highly favored of God.

Do you ever feel alone? Like everyone's against you? Let's find out what happens to people who are loved by God. Romans 8:31,32 says, *What shall we then say to these things? If God be for us, who can be against us? He that spared not his own son, but delivered him up for us all, how shall he not with him also, freely give us all things?*

There are a lot of Christians who are not convinced that God's for them. They think God's the enemy. How would you like to be commander-in-chief of an army where half of your troops don't even know who the enemy is? They've got their weapons pointed toward headquarters, blaming you all the time for their problems. It's like being commander-in-chief of a bunch of Gomer Pyles!

There are people questioning God, "Why did You let this happen to me?" They don't even realize that God is for them and not against them! God did not cause this awful situation in your life to prove something to you, He cares about you. You are so loved by God that He is willing to give you freely ALL things. He's on your side!

Verse 34 says, *Who is he that condemneth? It is Christ that died.* You shouldn't be walking in condemnation. You shouldn't be listening to the lies of the Devil condemning you all the time and telling you how lousy you are, what a failure and a nobody you are. A person who listens to that all the time does not have a revelation of favor and honor.

You're so highly favored of the Lord that He says no weapon formed against you shall prosper. You've been justified in the sight of God. NOTHING can separate you from God's love!

Romans 8:38,39 says, *For I am persuaded, that neither death, nor life, nor angels, nor principalities, nor powers, nor things present, nor things to come, nor height, nor depth, nor any other creature, shall be able to separate us from the love of God, which is in Christ Jesus our Lord.*

When you become "persuaded" of just how loved you are, and just how valuable you are in the sight of God, then you can say what Paul said, "there is nothing that can separate me from the love of Christ. Not things present nor things to come." AMEN!

You are somebody special. Quit running yourself down. Quit talking ugly about yourself. Quit talking about what a failure you are. Don't run yourself down all the time. Don't talk about how unworthy you are. You are the handiwork of God. You are loved. You are highly favored of God.

Expect greater victories in your life because everything you set your hand to prospers! Don't get discouraged when a storm comes, because you know you're favored of God and somehow, someway God will turn it around! You are crowned with glory and honor.

Begin to expect preferential treatment simply because you are highly favored of God. It's fun walking in favor because you never know how God's going to work the thing out, you just know He is.

I remember years ago right after I accepted Jesus into my life, Carolyn and I heard that Brother Kenneth Hagin was going to be ministering in Tyler, Texas. We were so eager to learn more about God's Word, and we would listen to Brother Hagin's tapes and read his books all the time. So, by an act of faith, Carolyn and I drove a great distance to be in that meeting. I was so excited to hear Kenneth Hagin. I wanted to sit on the front row because I liked to watch every move Brother Hagin made.

When we got to the meeting, the place was already jam-packed. They were having to bring extra chairs in and were already filling up the aisles and the back with people. When we walked in, the man said, "Well, I don't know where we're going to seat you." And another man came up and said,

"Tell those four right there to come with me." He put our four chairs "in front" of the front row. I call that favor.

Now, I didn't go in there demanding a front row seat, but the favor of the Lord gave me one. Now, that may not be a big deal to you, but the Lord knew that it was the desire of our heart, and He gave it to us.

When you know that you are highly favored of God, then you expect to be the head and not the tail; above and not beneath! Psalm 84:11 says, *..no good thing will He withhold from them that walk uprightly.* It's God's will to bless you! When you're honored and favored by God, you can expect every need to be met.

I Chronicles 29:11,12 says, *Thine, O Lord, is the greatness, and the power, and the glory, and the victory, and the majesty: for all that is in the heaven and in the earth is thine; thine is the kingdom, O Lord, and thou art exalted as head above all. (12) Both riches and honour come of thee, and thou reignest over all; and in thine hand is power and might; and in thine hand it is to make great, and to give strength unto all.*

Notice a link between riches and honor, financial success and stability. Prosperity is linked to honor. In other words, you will succeed financially when you walk in the favor of God.

Please don't get the impression that I'm saying, "If you walk in favor, you'll never have any more problems." I'm not saying that at all in fact, every revelation you receive from God, you will be held accountable for walking in it. It will produce the good fight of faith. Paul said, because of the abundance of revelation that was given unto me, a messenger of Satan was also sent to buffet me.

People who walk in an abundance of revelation also encounter an abundance of adversity. BUT when you know you walk in the favor of God, then praise God, you know that favor will carry you through the adversity and you will become victorious on the other side.

Right now, I urge you to allow the Holy Spirit to cleanse you from all the lies that Satan has put in your mind of worthlessness, insecurity and low self-esteem. You now have an understanding of who you are in Christ! You are crowned with glory and honor and you are somebody who is so special to God! I encourage you to make this confession right now:

"In the Name of Jesus by the authority of God's Word, from this moment forward, I do not look at myself in the natural but according to the Word of God. I see myself the way God sees me. I am highly favored of the Lord. I am crowned with glory and honor. I take authority over condemnation, guilt, shame, and inferiority - that's not of God. I break its power over me in Jesus' Name. I declare by faith, I have preferential treatment.

"From this moment forward, my self-esteem and my self-image shall rise and be in accordance to God's Word. I'll not be high-minded, I walk in humility, but I know who I am in Christ, and I fully expect the treatment that is afforded to those who are highly favored, in Jesus' Name. Every morning when I rise, I will declare this is the day the Lord has made, I will rejoice and be glad in it. TODAY I expect the favor of God to go before me in Jesus' Name. I'm honored by My Father, I am the object of His affection. And if God loves me, nothing can separate me from His love. I am somebody special to God in Jesus' Name." Amen.

For those who don't know Jesus, would you like to know Him?

If you were to die today, where would you spend eternity? If you have accepted Jesus Christ as your personal Lord and Savior, you can be assured that when you die, you will go directly into the presence of God in Heaven. If you have not accepted Jesus as your personal Lord and Savior, is there any reason why you can't make Jesus the Lord of your life right now? Please pray this prayer out loud, and as you do, pray with a sincere and trusting heart, and you will be born again.

Dear God in Heaven,

I come to you in the Name of Jesus to receive salvation and eternal life. I believe that Jesus is Your Son.

I believe that He died on the cross for my sins, and that You raised Him from the dead. I receive Jesus now into my heart and make Him the Lord of my life. Jesus, come into my heart. I welcome you as my Lord and Savior. Father, I believe Your Word that says I am now saved. I confess with my mouth that I am saved and born again. I am now a child of God.

Dr. Jerry Savelle is a noted author, evangelist, and teacher who travels extensively throughout the United States, Canada, and around the globe. He is president of Jerry Savelle Ministries International, a ministry of many outreaches devoted to meeting the needs of believers all over the world.

Well-known for his balanced Biblical teaching, Dr. Savelle has conducted seminars, crusades and conventions for over twenty-five years and has ministered in thousands of churches and fellowships. He is in great demand today because of his inspiring message of victory and faith and his vivid, and often humorous, illustrations from the Bible. He teaches the uncompromised Word of God with a power and an authority that is exciting, but with a love that delivers the message directly to the spirit man.

In addition to his international headquarters in Crowley, Texas, Dr. Savelle is also founder of JSMI Africa, JSMI United Kingdom, JSMI South Africa and JSMI Tanzania. In 1994, he established the JSMI Bible Institute and School of World Evangelism. It is a two-year school for the preparation of ministers to take the Gospel of Jesus Christ to the nations of the world.

The missions outreach of his ministry extends to over 50 countries around the world. JSMI further ministers the Word of God through its prison ministry outreach.

Dr. Savelle has authored many books and has an extensive video and cassette teaching tape ministry and a nation-wide television broadcast. Thousands of books, tapes, and videos are distributed around the world each year through Jerry Savelle Ministries International.

For a complete list of
tapes, books, and videos
by Jerry Savelle
write or call:

Jerry Savelle Ministries
International
P.O. Box 748
Crowley, TX 76036
(817) 297-3155